You put _____ **socks** _____ on your **feet** _____ .

feet   socks   valley   sneeze

_____ is the _____ before June.

spray   raise   May   month

Jean _____ a story to _____ .

bee   reads   Gail   bait

You _____ with your _____ .

gray   ears   beneath   hear

Lee drank a _____ of _____ .

feet   who   glass   water

The whale lives in the sea, but it is not a fish. It is a mammal, just like dogs, cats, and people, and it is the biggest mammal alive. Mammals don't breathe with gills, the way fish do. They have lungs to breathe with. Like other mammals, the whale has a big brain, and its babies get milk from the mother. Whales have some hair on them, too, but not as much as most other mammals have.

Whales are huge—between fifteen and a hundred feet long. Their thick blubber, or fat, keeps them from getting cold in the sea, and their flat tails help them to steer and swim. Whales can see and hear well. They have a way of speaking to each other in whistles, too.

The humpback whale is about fifty feet long. It is black on top, white underneath, and has long flippers. This kind of whale stays fairly near the shore, where it eats mostly small fish.

Who breathes with gills?

__Fish_____ breathe with gills.

Whales   (Fish)   People   Humpbacks

What is the size of the humpback whale?

It is _____ feet long.

a hundred   fifty   fifteen   five hundred

"Class, I want you to meet Kay Parker," said Dee's teacher, Mrs. Dean. "Kay is blind, and she is going to be in this class for reading."

Dee and the other children said "hi" to Kay. Then Dee raised her hand.

"Excuse me." She began to speak, waited, then went on. "I don't mean to be mean," Dee said, "but can Kay read if she can't see?"

"I'm glad you asked," said Mrs. Dean. "Help me explain, Kay."

Kay picked up a book and held it up for the class to see.

"Kay doesn't read the way you children read. She doesn't look at letters on the page. She reads Braille. Pages written in Braille have small raised dots or bumps on them. The dots are like letters. Blind people 'read' the dots by feeling them with the tips of their fingers. Today Kay will read the same story we do, but she will read it in Braille."

Kay rubbed her fingers along the first line and told the children what it said.

"That's neat," said Dee. "Will you teach us, Kay?"

What is the main idea?

Mrs. Dean is blind.　　　Dee reads to Kay.

(Kay reads Braille.)　　　Dee teaches Braille to Kay.

Kay reads Braille.

Dean was carrying Kitty the kitten home from the pet store. Kitty was afraid. She twisted and wriggled and scratched until Dean had to let go of her, and then—whee!—she got away and streaked down the street.

"Mmm—good!" she said, raising her nose in the air. "I smell fish!" She trailed the smell to an old pail of bait behind Mr. Carver's fish store. She knocked the pail over, ate some of the bait, and then rolled in the rest. Did she smell bad! Then she scampered off, leaving a trail of fishy smell behind her.

In the next block, Mrs. Heath was painting a chair white.

"Yummy! I need some milk," Kitty said when she saw the bucketful of white stuff. She ran up to the pail and dipped her nose in. But Mrs. Heath saw her, screamed, and jumped—and as she did she spilled the paint all over Kitty. Kitty ran away, but she had paint all over her, and she left a trail of white paint dripping behind her.

Meanwhile, Dean trailed the fishy smell and the paint tracks. When Kitty had her nose in a trash can, Dean reached out and grabbed her.

"I'm glad you made a mess," he told her, "so I was able to find you."

What is the main idea?
    ✓ Kitty runs away.   ___ Kitty steals an eagle.

1, 2, 3, 4, or X?

__2__ Kitty eats the bait.   __1__ Kitty jumps out of Dean's hands.

__X__ Kitty licks Dean.   __3__ Kitty dips her nose in the paint.

__4__ Dean catches Kitty.   __X__ The kitten rolls in the paint.

Mr. Smith _____ the van onto the _____ .

street   steers   sleep   strain

A _____ is on the _____ .

afraid   stairs   raise   nail

The branch of the _____ bends in the _____ .

need   tree   breeze   tray

The kitten has a _____ _____ .

greet   gray   say   tail

The ice _____ was good to _____ .

sweet   leash   cream   eat

Jean and her three older sisters are camping in a clearing by a stream. Jean's sisters are twelve, fifteen, and sixteen years old. Jean is just nine. As the sun begins to set, Jean begins to feel afraid. She hears the peepers croaking by the stream, and the trees creaking in the wind.

"What if a wild animal comes?" asks Jean.

"There are no animals here but deer, and they are afraid of <u>you</u>," says Dee. "Put your sleeping bag between Dee's and mine, and you will be safe," adds Gail, the oldest.

"Snuggle into your sleeping bag and I will tell you a bedtime story," says the twelve-year-old, Kay.

Kay begins to tell a funny story about the Peanut Butter Fairy. Jean giggles a lot, and by the time Kay has nearly reached the end of the story, she is asleep.

What is Jean's age?   Jean is _____

_____

_____ years old.

nine   three   fifteen

Where are the sisters camping?   They are camping _____

_____

_____ .

near a peanut   in a tree house   by a stream

"Brr! It's cold today and I hate winter," said Gail as she swept the driveway. She breathed in the crisp, fall air as the leaves rustled beneath her feet.

When the driveway was clear, she sat down near the beech tree in a big heap of leaves Dad had raked.

"At least I don't have to admit that it's winter until the last leaf has fallen from the trees," she said.

She looked up at the branches. They seemed black and bare against the pale gray sky. Nearly all the leaves had fallen from the trees, but one lone leaf was left hanging from the end of a branch, swaying in the breeze.

Then a strong gust of wind began to shake the tree and chase the fallen leaves. The leaf flapped in the wind, still clinging to its branches.

"Oh, please don't fall!" prayed Gail, as she watched the leaf. But then the strongest gust of all was too much for the leaf. It fluttered to and fro, then landed in Gail's lap.

What is the main idea?

Gail likes to be cold.	Winter begins for Gail.
It is springtime for Gail.	Gail hates playing in leaves.

The red team and the white team are playing baseball in the lot near Greg's house. Greg, who is on the red team, is up at bat. The first pitch is too wide, and the next two are too close to Greg.

"Three balls!" thinks Greg. "Maybe I'll get walked to first base."

Greg hits the next pitch onto the grass near the pitcher and runs as fast as he can to first base. The pitcher runs to get the ball, but Greg's dog, who has been watching the game from the gate, runs faster and picks up the ball in his teeth. The pitcher is upset that he can't get the ball. "No fair!" he yells.

The dog runs to Greg and drops the ball at his feet. By this time, Greg is near first base, and he keeps going. The ball goes between Greg and the first base man. The first base man grabs the ball and tags Greg.

"Out!" yells the pitcher.

Greg walks over and pats his dog. "Nice catch," he tells him, "but you helped the wrong team."

What is the main idea?
___ Greg's dog helps the red team.   ___ The dog helps the white team.

1, 2, 3, 4, or X?
_____ The dog grabs the ball.   _____ Greg strikes out.

_____ Greg has a hit.   _____ The dog drops the ball.

_____ Greg grabs the ball.   _____ The first base man tags Greg.

Jean is _____ _____ old.

train   pay   sixteen   years

It _____ on the _____ .

seen   rained   plain   pail

Dad ate _____ and _____ .

jeeps   beans   peas   seats

Kathy's long _____ goes down to her _____ .

hear   weep   waist   hair

The _____ graze on the _____ grass.

sheep   green   pain   speak

Dean dives under a wave just in time, but Kay doesn't see it coming so she gets knocked over. They are both giggling as the wave ebbs back into the sea.

"I'll race you up the beach!" yells Kay, and the two children run off at top speed.

Meanwhile, Mom is walking down the beach with Bobby, hunting for seashells and collecting them in a pail. Bobby kneels down and picks up something from the seaweed.

"Look at this one, Mom!" he says. "It's shiny blue and silver."

"That's a mussel," Mom tells him. "They are good to eat."

While all this is going on, Dad is sitting in a beach chair reading and watching little Andy running around in the sand, chasing seagulls.

At last it is time to go home.

"Shake all the sand off your feet before you get in the van," Dad tells the children. "We don't want to bring the beach home with us."

"Why not?" jokes Dean. "That seems like a good idea to me!"

_____

What does Bobby pick up?   He picks up _____

_____

_____ .

seaweed   a green shell   the reef   a mussel

Who plays with Dean?   _____

_____

_____ plays with Dean.

Kay   Bobby   Dad   Andy

"My ice cream cone is better than yours," says Gail, trying to make Lee mad. "It's real peach!" The two children are walking home in the hot sun.

Lee wants to ignore his sister. The cherry ice cream is dripping down the sides of his cone, and he keeps licking as fast as he can.

Gail doesn't give up. "Mine is bigger than yours, too," she nags.

Lee still wants to ignore her, but he is getting mad. He sees that her cone is bigger than his. "That's not fair!" he says. "Yours is bigger."

Gail sticks her nose up in the air. "You just eat yours faster than I do. I like to save mine as long as I can."

Lee is angry. He doesn't like being outdone by his sister, so he stops eating. As soon as they reach home, he sneaks into the kitchen and puts his ice cream in the freezer. Gail comes into the kitchen, gobbling up the last bite of her cone.

Lee smiles at her. "I still have the rest of my cone left," he tells her, "and I can save it for as long as I want. It's in the freezer!"

What is the main idea?

Gail's cone lasts longer than Lee's.　　The man gave Lee less ice cream than Gail.

Lee's ice cream drips.　　Lee and Gail eat ice cream cones.

_____

_____

_____

_____

"What are you doing?" asked Janey when she walked into the kitchen and saw her oldest sister standing by the stove.

"Mom and Dad got married fifteen years ago today," said Patsy, "so I told them I'd make dinner."

"Neat! Can I help?" Janey asked. She grabbed an egg beater from the drying rack on the sink.

Patsy smiled and told her sister gently, "Yes, you can help, but we don't need eggs beaten. First get a tray and take the cheese and crackers in to Mom and Dad."

Eager to help, Janey carried the tray into the den. Meanwhile, Patsy peeked at the beef and checked the green beans and rice on the top of the stove. They were not quite done.

Janey came running back to the kitchen. "This is fun, making dinner. Let's have cake and ice cream first!"

"Sweet things come *after* dinner," Patsy explained. "Let's take out the beef."

What is the main idea?
    __ Patsy beats the eggs.   __ Patsy and Janey make dinner.

1, 2, 3, 4, or X?

_____ Janey liked to eat peas.   _____ Janey grabbed an egg beater.

_____ Janey asked for cake and ice   _____ Janey carried the tray.

      cream.

_____ Patsy checked the beef and

      beans.

The _____ has _____ to help her.

jail   maids   way   queen

My bike _____ is made of _____ .

steel   cheer   chain   dream

A _____ is longer than a _____ .

pair   week   day   freeze

The _____ is _____ of the hunter.

paid   brain   deer   afraid

The _____ has six _____ .

read   wheels   cheek   trailer

Kay and her English sheep dog, Heath, walk into the kitchen, where Mom is making lunch. Mom screams when she sees that all the dog's hair has been shaved off. Heath sits down and begins to scratch his ears with his hind foot.

"What did they do to him?" she asks.

"The vet shaved him so the fleas can't hide in his long hair. We have to treat him with this stuff three times a day," says Kay, handing Mom the spray bottle.

"OK," Mom tells her, "let's get it over with. You hold the leash, and I'll wash."

Outside, Mom kneels down and sprays the flea bath on the dog. Then she scrubs him with a sponge and rinses him off with the hose.

"That stuff smells really bad," says Kay.

"Yes," says Mom, "but it kills those nasty fleas."

Why did the dog go to the vet?   The dog has _____

_____

_____ .

long hair   a bad sprain   painful feet   fleas

What kind of dog does Kay have?   She has an _____

_____

_____ .

mutt   English setter   English sheep dog   collie

"Let's get a jeep!" Lee said to her father as they walked by a place that sold jeeps.

"I don't think so," said Dad. "They're not what we need."

"But Dad, they have 4-wheel drive, so they can go on steep trails and ride on the sand at the beach. They can drag things out of the mud or pull trailers behind them. And on some jeeps you can take the top off and have a fun, breezy ride! Let's get one, please!"

"We don't need to go on steep trails or sandy beaches," Dad explained. "We need something bigger, like a van, that can carry all 7 of us. Besides, the ride is too bumpy in a jeep."

What is the main idea?

Jeeps have seatbelts.   Lee wants a jeep.

Dad wants a jeep.   Jeeps have wheels.

_____

_____

_____

_____

Gail had her friend Kay over to dinner. At the end of the meal, Gail got up from her chair and said, "Excuse me. I have to go upstairs to floss and brush my teeth. I'll be back."

"That's a really good idea," said Kay. "Can I come, too? I need to take better care of my teeth."

"Fine. Come on!" agreed Gail.

The two of them went upstairs and got the dental floss from the shelf. As she was pulling the floss out of its case, Gail explained, "Since I went to the dentist I've been doing this after I eat."

"I need to do that, too," said Kay. "Then maybe I won't need to get any fillings."

What is the main idea?
__ Kay and Gail have bad teeth.　　　　__ Kay and Gail floss their teeth.

1, 2, 3, 4, or X?
_____ They get the dental floss.　　　　_____ They floss their teeth.

_____ They go upstairs.　　　　_____ Gail chips her front teeth.

_____ Gail and Kay eat dinner.　　　　_____ Kay goes to the dentist.

The _____ can _____ in the pond.

throat   boat   float   beat

You _____ with _____ .

soap   clean   steep   clay

I like to _____ my _____ with jam.

coat   toast   crow   eat

The _____ is next to the _____ .

sidewalk   read   throw   road

Mrs. Heath said, "_____ at that _____ !"

least   deer   Look   low

"Don't go to the Witch House!" Danny tells Hank and Dee. "It's really scary!" They are at the fair.

"I'm not afraid," says Hank. "Neither am I," adds Dee.

Dee and Hank get in their seats on the little train. As the train rolls down the track into the Witch House, the track begins to creak. Then, suddenly, all is black. The children hear screams and then a wicked cackle. The train stops and a huge, creepy witch appears near where Dee and Hank are sitting—<u>too near</u>! She has a green face and long, matted hair. Her hair and her ragged dress are full of cobwebs, and bats are clinging to her sleeve. The witch puts out her hands as if to grab the children. The bats squeak. Dee screams, and Hank almost jumps out of his seat.

Just then the train begins to go again. Hank is still breathing fast, and Dee can't speak by the time the train gets back outside. Danny is waiting by the steps.

"See what I mean?" he asks.

_____

Who screams in the Witch House? _____

_____

_____ screams.

Danny   Hank   Dee   The witch

Where are the bats?   They are on the _____

_____

_____

train   children   witch's waist   witch's sleeve

It was a cold, gray, rainy day in the middle of the summer.

"I hate days like this," Max said to his sister, as they walked home from the trolley stop.

"Not me," said Bev. "I'd like it to stay like this all year."

"Why?" asked Max. "Don't you like the sunshine?"

"Yes," said Bev, "but I hate the heat, and that heat wave we had last week was too much. I was so hot I was beat. All I did that whole week was sit near the fan and drink mint tea with ice. But when it rains, it is not as hot so I don't mind staying home. Then I can read or play or take a nap or chat on the phone."

"I don't agree," said Max. "I like to stay outside and ride around on my bike all day. I don't care if it reaches a hundred, as long as it's not raining."

What is the main idea?

Max and Bev chat about the heat.   Max likes the rain.

It is a hot day.   Dee likes to drink iced tea.

_____

_____

_____

_____

"What a bad day this has been," said Mrs. Heath to her husband, as she came home from her job as a beekeeper.

"Lots of things went wrong. I can't wait to sit down, put my feet up, and rest."

With her jacket still on, she plopped herself down on the old green easy chair. CRUNCH!! The left leg of the chair was weak, and it broke. As Mrs. Heath fell on her knees she snapped, "I told you this was a bad day for me, and it doesn't seem to be getting much better!"

By the time her husband reached her, Mrs. Heath was leaning on the side of the chair and smiling. "Look what was behind the chair—the ring I lost last year! Today hasn't been such a bad day after all!"

What is the main idea?
— Mrs. Heath had a lucky day.   — Mrs. Heath had a bad day.

1, 2, 3, 4, or X?
_____ Mrs. Heath sat on her husband.   _____ Mrs. Heath came home.

_____ The chair broke.   _____ Mrs. Heath saw her ring.

_____ Mrs. Heath napped in the chair.   _____ Mrs. Heath sat in the chair.

Joan has new _____ for her _____ .

owe   boat   fear   oars

You have ten _____ on your _____ .

glow   feet   toes   loaf

The _____ will _____ the baseball.

load   throw   pitcher   roast

Joan _____ Mom her new _____ .

coat   grow   showed   toe

An _____ tree will _____ to be big.

oak   grow   flow   hoe

"Look!" said Mom, as she and her children drove by the school down the street. "Those kids are doing a May Pole dance."

"What's that?" asked Ray.

Mom stopped the car. "On the first day of May, or May Day, people dance around the May Pole to welcome spring," she explained. "See the pink and green streamers pinned to the top of the pole? As people dance in a circle around the pole, they are weaving the streamers together like a braid."

"Why does that woman in the white dress have daisies in her hair?" asked Sally.

"It looks like she's the May Queen," Mom told her.

"I think they need a May King, too," said Ray.

_____

Who has daisies in her hair? _____

_____

_____ has daisies in her hair.

The Princess   The May Queen   Mom   Sally

What is pinned to the May Pole? _____

_____

_____ are pinned to the May Pole.

Children   Blossoms   Streamers   Baskets

Dad said to Kate and Bill, "Today I'm going to teach you to use a hammer." He gave each of them a hammer and a block of pine. Then he told them, "Pick up the hammer in one hand and hold it at the end."

Next Dad gave each of them a nail. He said, "Hold the nail here with your other hand, like this. Keep your fingers at the base of the nail. Then tap the top with the hammer. Just keep on tapping until the nail goes in deep. But do not try to hammer too fast, and be careful to hit the nail, not your fingers!"

Just then, Kate sneezed. Dad smiled at her. "I'm glad you didn't do that while you were trying to hammer," he said.

What is the main idea?

The kids have blocks of pine.　　Dad hammers the chair.

Dad teaches the kids to hammer.　　Kate sneezes.

While Mrs. Heath is upstairs drying her hair with the hair dryer, a robber is sneaking into her house. Mrs. Heath doesn't hear him. He piles all the things he wants into a big heap in the hall—a pair of gold candlesticks, a silver tray, the VCR, a heater, and—biggest of all—the TV.

It is too much for the robber to carry, but he is greedy, so he keeps trying. He has just picked up the last thing and is about to leave when he drops the TV. BANG!! It lands on his feet, and he screams at the top of his lungs!

This time she hears the robber. She runs to the phone and calls the cops.

Meanwhile, the robber begins to limp away, but by the time he reaches the end of the driveway the cops are there.

"You'll have to come with us," says one cop as the other takes the robber's arm.

What is the main idea?
 __ A robber comes to Mrs. Heath's house.   __ The robber gets a new TV.

1, 2, 3, 4, or X?
 _____ The cops get the robber.   _____ Mrs. Heath calls the cops.

 _____ Mrs. Heath grabs the robber.   _____ The robber grabs the cops.

 _____ The robber drops the TV.   _____ The robber picks up the TV.

The _____ is _____ of oatmeal.

bowl   full   tow   peel

The _____ truck is very _____ .

toad   bow   slow   tow

Joe _____ the grass so it is _____ .

meal   row   low   mows

The _____ has a huge _____ .

throat   toad   steam   reach

At _____ we need _____ to see.

light   load   fight   night

A toad is like a frog, but the frog is thinner and has longer legs. Toads have no tails and they have very thick, bumpy skin. Glands in the bumpy skin make something that toads can spray on you. It can make you sick.

Toads can't hop as well as frogs. Frogs jump or hop to get away if they are being chased, but toads just sit there.

Toads sleep in the daytime and eat bugs when the sun goes down. Most of the time toads live on land, but they lay eggs in ponds, and the eggs hatch into tadpoles.

_____

When does the toad sleep?   The toad sleeps _____

_____

_____ .

in the summer   at ten o'clock   when the sun sets   in the daytime

Where does the toad lay eggs? The toad lays eggs _____

_____

_____ .

in a hen house   on the land   in the pond   under a tree

The king and queen were happy. They had a huge castle, each other, and—best of all—they had one child, Princess Daisy, with long hair, soft skin, and a sweet, sunny smile that made you think of daisies. The king always felt happy when he saw the princess.

Then, one gray day, the queen passed away. The king was so sad that he didn't want to see people. He locked himself in one place and wept for weeks and weeks. He was so sad that he forgot about Princess Daisy. She wanted to share the sadness with him but he kept himself locked up and didn't see her.

Princess Daisy was sad, too, but she had hope. Each day she leaned out the window and prayed for the king to get better. Each night a daisy began to grow in the grass below her window, until there were well over a hundred daisies outside the castle.

One day, the king, in all his sadness, happened to look out and there he saw the daisies. "Princess Daisy!" he said to himself. "I must see her!"

He called for the princess, and they hugged and hugged. The more he looked at her hopeful, happy face, the better he felt. "I miss the queen," he told her, "but I am so lucky to have you!"

What is the main idea?

Princess Daisy was angry.   The king hated daisies.

The princess had long hair.   The princess helped the king.

Dee saw Dad in the van, sweeping the seat with a dust pan and brush. "What are you doing, Dad?" asked Dee.

"I'm sweeping up cat hair," he told her.

"What is cat hair doing on the seat?" she asked.

"It's Kitty's. Each winter, cats grow long hair to keep them from getting too cold. It's called their winter coat. Then, in the spring, they don't need that long hair, so it drops off. That's called shedding. Kitty leaves tufts of her winter coat in places where she has been. Look. You can tell that she was sleeping here on the back seat."

"I bet I know another place where she has been sleeping. There is cat hair on my bed, too. I'm going to find Kitty."

What is the main idea?

___ Dee has long hair.　　　　___ The cat is shedding.

1, 2, 3, 4, or X?

_____ Dee saw Dad.　　　　_____ Dad swept the seat.

_____ Dee went to find Kitty.　　　　_____ Dad cut Dee's hair.

_____ Dad sweeps Dee's bed.　　　　_____ Dad told Dee about shedding.

The dump truck has a _____ of _____ .

bow   snow   load   glow

The _____ is _____ to the boat.

loaf   hoe   flying   crow

Joan has a _____ in her _____ .

hopeful   bow   bowling   hair

The _____ can _____ on the lake.

boat   helpful   low   float

The sun's _____ is too _____ .

bright   light   right   tight

Fruit grows in many places. Apples, peaches, plums, and cherries grow on trees. Most berries—like raspberries, blueberries, and blackberries—grow on bushes, and cranberries grow on vines in low, wet places like bogs or swamps. Grapes grow on vines, too, but in dry, high places.

Fruit grows year after year, so the people who grow it don't have to keep planting seeds again each spring. But fruit growers do have to take good care of the plants. The plants have to be pruned each year to cut back the weak branches. People need to feed the fruit to kill insects. Otherwise, insects will be more likely to eat the fruit.

Fruit is good to eat and good for you, too. It tastes good all by itself or made into pies, crumblers, juice, fruit cup, fruitcake, or ice cream.

Did you know that nuts are fruit, too?

_____

What is pruning?   Pruning means _____

_____

_____ .

eating   growing   cutting   spraying

Where do cranberries grow?   They grow in _____

_____

_____ .

swamps   trees   dry places   bushes

It had been raining all day, but the sky was slowly beginning to clear. On one side of the house it was sunny, and on the other side it was drizzling.

"Let's go outside," Dad told Kay, "and see if there's a rainbow."

"Neat!" said Kay.

They walked out the back door, and there it was against the gray sky—a huge, bright rainbow.

"Dad, you were right. What made you think there might be a rainbow?"

"Rainbows sometimes appear when the sun shines on raindrops in the air, so there must be rain and sunshine at the same time."

What is the main idea?

The sky was clearing.   The rainbow is all blue.

Dad and Kay see a rainbow.   The rainbow grows on the door.

"This is the place where I most like to be," says Joan to her friend, "—the coast of Maine. It makes me feel so peaceful." She breathes deeply to smell the pine trees, then looks all around her.

Below, on the flat rocks, a seagull is strutting about looking for some dinner. She hears a putt-putt sound. A lobsterman steers his boat carefully in the cove. He is checking his traps to see if he has gotten some lobsters. He pulls the rope holding a trap and finds one big green lobster inside.

Joan hears a splash off the rocks and looks to see the seagull diving for a fish for dinner. Then she hears a smaller splash out on the bay. It's fish leaping into the air, hunting for insects to eat.

Joan leans back against a tree. "It was really fun today in my uncle's sailboat," she says to her friend. "We saw some seals out on a ledge, and on the way home some dolphins followed us for a while."

"There is just one animal I still want to see—a puffin," her friend says.

What is the main idea?

   —   Joan likes Maine.   —   Joan wants a pet seagull.

1, 2, 3, 4, or X?

_____   A seagull takes a dive.   _____   Joan smells the pines.

_____   Joan splashes in the bay.   _____   She sees a lobster boat.

_____   Some fish jump in the bay.   _____   Joan's dad has a sailboat.

_____   _____

_____ had a _____ with his sister.

fight   blue   fries   Joe

_____   _____

_____ mom is a _____ .

woman   Sue's   pie   glue

_____   _____

Dad put on a _____   _____ .

blue   spies   tie   cried

_____   _____

Jeff likes to _____ French _____ .

die   true   eat   fries

_____   _____

Is it _____ that you made a _____ ?

dries   pie   true   due

Joe woke up wheezing and sneezing. He had a scratchy sore throat that felt most painful when he swallowed, and his nose was stuffed up.

Joe groaned. "I can't be sick! Today's my first hockey game!" He sniffled, then gave his nose a good blow and felt his cheeks. They felt hot, and he felt like he was going to faint, so he asked his mother to take a look at him.

"It seems to be the flu," she told him, feeling his cheeks. "I know you wanted to play in the game, but you'd better stay in bed, get plenty of rest, and drink lots of juice."

Joe lay down on his bed. He was upset to be missing the game. "But I can tell I really am sick, so I can't be much help to my teammates when I'm like this," he said to himself. "Well, at least I can read and watch TV."

_____

Where is Joe's mom?   She is _____

_____

_____ .

at home   at a hockey game   on the phone   at her desk

What is wrong with Joe?   He seems to have _____

_____

_____ .

a sprain   the flu   a mild cold   an infected cut

Eels are long, thin fish that are shaped like snakes and have wet, slippery, thin skin. Some eels have scales on their skin. But unlike snakes, they have flat tails. Most eels live in the sea, but some live in streams.

Grown eels are between three and six feet long. In the fall of the year, eels swim from their homes in the streams down to the sea to breed. After they lay their eggs there, they die. Next spring, the little eels appear. At about one year old, the eels swim back upstream. They grow up there until it is time to breed.

Some people like to catch eels for eating; some people catch small sand eels for bait. One way they get them is by putting out nets and trapping them when the eels swim downstream to breed. Another way people catch eels is by spearing them in shallow or muddy places in streams.

What is the main idea?

Eels live on land.   Eels are a kind of fish.

Eels are three inches long.   Eels have scales.

_____

_____

_____

_____

It is Joe's first time playing in a hockey game. His friend passes him the puck. Joe gets the puck and speeds for the goal. He is thinking about making a goal, so he barely hears the people cheering for him.

He pulls back his hockey stick and hits the puck. Wham! The puck slides fast on the ice, but the goalie nabs it and passes it to one of his teammates. Joe is skating so fast that he skids right into the goal post.

"Try again!" yells Joe's coach. Joe's friend steals the puck from the other team and again passes it to Joe. Again Joe aims at the goal, but this time it slides a bit to the side of the goalie. The goalie comes out to kick the puck, but misses.

It happens like lightning. The puck flies by the goalie and lodges in the net at the back of the goal.

The people roar! Joe's teammates skate over and pat him on the back. Joe has made his first goal in his first game.

What is the main idea?

    ___ Joe misses the goal.   ___ Joe makes a goal.

1, 2, 3, 4, or X?

_____ Joe's teammates pat him.   _____ Joe's friend makes a goal.

_____ Joe's coach yells.   _____ The goalie gets the puck.

_____ The goalie misses the puck.   _____ Joe cracks the goal post.

The little _____ _____ _____ its wings.

clue   either   bluejay   tries

Mick waited until the _____ _____ .

flow   dried   glue   where

The _____ is _____ up in the sky.

high   airplane   clue   elbow

_____ is five days _____ Sunday.

before   lie   Tuesday   bruise

A _____ is a kind of _____ .

fuel   blueberry   cries   fruit

"My cat has six toes on one of her feet," Ben tells his friend, Jay.

"I bet you made that up," replies Jay. "You don't have to make things up to impress me."

"I'm not lying!" insists Ben. "It's really true! I'll get my cat and show you." He hurries out of the den to find her.

"Willow!" he calls. "Here, Willow!" But the cat is not around so he can't show Jay her toes. Ben walks back to the den. As he passes the stairs he sees that a bottle of paint has spilled on the floor.

"What's that doing there?" he asks himself. When he inspects it more closely, he sees the cat's tracks in the paint. One of the tracks has six spots where her six toes stepped.

"Jay!" yells Ben. "Come here! I can't find Willow, but here's a clue!"

_____

What does Ben find?   Ben finds a _____

_____

_____ .

cat   track   willow   big toe

Where is the paint?   It is on the _____

_____

_____ .

train track   den   door   floor

"Do you hear the peepers?" Joan asked her friend Ann as they waited for the sun to set.

"What do you mean, peepers?" replied Ann.

"Peepers are the animals making that high Peep-Peep-Peep down by the stream. Another name for them is tree toads. They are little toads who leap from tree to tree. They have sticky pads on the bottoms of their feet so they don't fall.

"In the spring, at dusk, you can hear them going 'Peep! Peep! Peep! Peep!' That's the males calling the females. Their throats swell up like a bubble about to pop. The air coming out of their throats makes that peep.

"I like hearing the first peepers. It makes me think spring is here and we can spend more time outside. It means that school will be out before long."

_____

What is the main idea?

Peepers have sticky feet.   Joan explains about peepers.

The peepers are fighting.   Peepers pop bubbles.

_____

_____

_____

_____

Most of the time Joe wore blue jeans, but on Tuesday night he had a date, so he wanted to get dressed up. He had a bath and washed his hair. After the bath, he shaved, patted some after-shave on his cheeks, and brushed his teeth. Then he put on his blue suit with a bright yellow striped tie.

His sister Jean was in the hall when Joe came out of his room. She squealed when she saw him. "What a handsome sight! Do I know you?"

"Don't tease me," Joe said as he put on his gray raincoat and began to leave.

"I'm not teasing," she told him. "I mean it. You look really good."

Joe floated out of the house, dreaming of his date. "Maybe I really <u>do</u> look good," he said to himself.

What is the main idea?

—   Joe made his bed.   —   Joe got dressed up.

1, 2, 3, 4, or X?

_____   Joe cleaned himself up.   _____   Joe floated out of the house.

_____   He put on his raincoat.   _____   He has a yellow cloak.

_____   He put on a suit and tie.

The black _____ buzzed near the _____ .

    pie   flies   duel   cruise

The wet _____ _____ in the sun.

    cries   dries   clue   coat

The stream _____ very _____ .

    Tuesday   slowly   flows   tie

Mom goes _____ on _____ .

    throat   bowling   Tuesday   tow

You can go either up _____ down _____ .

    or   stairs   float   lie

41

"Look out the side window!" yelled Ray, as he and his father were driving one day. "There's a funny-looking truck driving slowly down the middle of the road. What's it doing? Are they cleaning the street?"

"No," Dad told him. "See the pail of paint on the back bumper? The truck is painting white lines on the road."

"Why?" asked Ray. He hadn't seen lines on the street before.

Dad explained. "Lines on the road help drivers. They show us what lane to drive in. You have to stay on the right side of the lines. When there are lines side by side, it means no passing there, but a dotted line shows a place where it's all right to pass."

"What if a truck drives on the line before the paint dries?" asked Ray.

"The paint they use is fast-drying," said Dad, "but that does happen sometimes. Then you have a messy line in the middle of the road."

What do two lines on the road mean?   They mean _____

_____

_____ .

pass here   drive slowly   no passing   drive fast

Where was the pail of paint?   It was on the _____

_____

_____ .

dotted line   bumper   road   tow truck

42

Joan had lunch at Neil's house on Tuesday. "I'm going up in an airplane for the first time on Sunday. What was it like when you went in one? Were you afraid?"

"No," Neil told her. "It was fun. Try to sit by a window. Then you can look out and see the roads and houses beneath you. The plane is up so high that big trucks look like little ants, and you can hardly see the people at all. When you look at the land and streams and coastline from an airplane, it's like looking at a map. It's quite a sight."

"I'm still a little afraid," Joan said.

"I bet you will really like it," said Neil. "There was just one thing I didn't like. When the plane lands, it can be really bumpy, so don't forget to keep your seat belt on. If you do get scared, do some deep breathing."

What is the main idea?

Neil tells about flying in an airplane.   Neil saw roads from the airplane.

Neil hated flying in an airplane.   Joan knows about fixing airplanes.

What comes out of frogs' eggs when they hatch in ponds in the spring? Not little frogs, but tadpoles.

You can catch tadpoles and watch them grow if you keep them in water. At first, they look more like little fish than frogs. They swim with fins and a tail, but they don't have legs yet. They don't have lungs to breathe with, but they have gills the way fish do. They eat plants that grow in the water.

Then, slowly, the tadpoles begin to grow. Their gills become lungs, and little stumps begin to bulge from their sides. These grow bigger and become legs and feet. As the tadpoles become grown-up frogs, they need long hind legs for swimming and for jumping on land. Grown-up frogs can catch insects to eat, and make croaking sounds with their big throats.

What is the main idea?
    — Tadpoles grow into frogs.   — Little frogs hatch from eggs.

1, 2, 3, 4, or X?

_____ Fish eat tadpoles.   _____ They grow legs.

_____ Tadpoles eat plants in ponds.   _____ Tadpoles hatch from eggs.

_____ Grown-up frogs breathe with gills.   _____ Grown-up frogs croak.

The _____ is not _____ .

cried   helpful   woman   dries

The _____ is black and _____ .

blue   ties   bruise   lie

The _____ in the cup is _____ .

show   sticky   true   glue

The child _____ to tie a _____ .

tries   bow   clue   glow

Dad squeezed _____ from the _____ .

cruise   suit   fruit   juice

Guppies are very little fish that live on the tops of ponds and streams, ditches and marshes. Most of the time they eat insects, but sometimes they eat little plants. Their fins can be red and blue or gray and pale green.

Guppies are easy to raise in a fish tank. They are strong, they breed lots of little guppies, and they can live for about three years unless they are unlucky. If the mother guppy gets quite hungry, she sometimes eats her offspring!

The female guppy is about three inches long, is gray and pale green, and swims slowly. The male is smaller, is red, blue, and green with black spots, and swims faster than the female.

_____

Where does the guppy live?   It lives in _____

_____

_____ .

dollhouses   the sea   streams   cages

What does the hungry female eat?   The female eats _____

_____

_____ .

her babies   the male   big fish   spots

Dad and Neil borrowed a rowboat to go on a fishing trip. Dad rowed out to the middle of the lake.

"Will you teach me to row?" asked Neil, before they began to fish.

"Hold an oar in each hand, and pull. Keep the paddle end of the oar in the water. The oar lock on the side of the boat helps hold the oar."

Neil got into the middle seat and began to row. "It's not as easy as it looks," he said, as he tried to pull on the two oars. Then one oar suddenly popped out of the oarlock. Neil was so surprised that he dropped the other oar into the pond. At first the oar looked like it was going to float. Then it slowly began to sink.

"Oh no!" yelled Dad. He dived into the lake and pulled up the oar. He handed it to Neil, and struggled back into the boat, soaking wet. "Maybe it's better for us to row where the water is shallower," said Neil.

What is the main idea?

The boat has two oarlocks.	The rowboat sank.
Neil can row quite well.	Neil tries to row the boat.

_____

_____

_____

_____

Kay's dad is teaching her to bowl. He begins to explain the game to her.

"Don't tell me about it," says Kay. "<u>Show</u> me." Dad picks up the bowling ball, holds it at his waist, takes three steps to the line on the floor, and lets go of the ball. The ball rolls down the lane and knocks down all ten pins.

"A strike!" yells Dad.

"Does that mean you're out?" asks Kay. Dad smiles. "No, that's baseball. A strike in bowling means you hit all ten pins with one ball. It's called a spare when you hit all ten pins with two tries."

"Can I try?" asks Kay. "It looks easy."

She picks up the ball. "Yikes!" she groans. "I hope I don't drop it on my toe!" She takes three steps, aims the ball, and throws. It rolls slowly down the alley and knocks down three pins.

"I didn't get a strike," Kay says sadly.

"Don't feel bad," says Dad. "You did well for a beginner. A lot of people can't roll the ball down the lane on their first try."

What is the main idea?

    __ Kay drops the ball on her toe.   __ Kay tries bowling.

1, 2, 3, 4, or X?

_____ Kay takes three steps.   _____ Kay gets a strike.

_____ Dad gets a strike.   _____ The ball hits three pins.

_____ Dad gets a spare.   _____ Kay picks up the ball.

Mom _____ , "Please _____ here."

said   arm   smart   come

Dad drives the _____ to the _____ lot.

spark   car   jar   parking

At sunset it _____ to get _____ .

dark   card   starts   barn

Your hand is at the _____ of your _____ .

far   arm   lie   end

The _____ are very _____ away.

far   park   stars   cried

It is snowing, and Mr. Sloan wants to get home from his job safely. He doesn't live far away, so he tries to drive home. The road is icy, and Mr. Sloan drives slowly, but the snow is getting deeper and deeper. It is snowing so hard that Mr. Sloan can hardly see the road as he drives around the corner.

Then the car gets stuck in the snow. Mr. Sloan gets out to look at the tires. He looks up and sees where he is.

"I'm stuck in the road next to my own driveway!" he says. "That's lucky!"

_____

Where does Mr. Sloan's car get stuck?   It gets stuck _____

_____

_____

far away   near his home   in the mud   in the rain

When does Mr. Sloan laugh?   Mr. Sloan laughs when he sees _____

_____

_____ .

the deep snow   the car's tires   his driveway   his job

One Sunday morning Bev sees the school band marching down North Street to the park. She likes the beat of the drum best, but when she sees her friend Sally in the front row playing the French horn, she thinks to herself, "I want to try that."

The next day at school, Bev sees Sally in the locker room. "Can I try to play your French horn?" she asks. "I might want to take lessons."

Sally nods, gets her horn out of her locker, and hands it to Bev.

"Here you go," she says. Bev tries to play while Sally is putting on her gym shorts. Bev's cheeks puff out and she gets red, but not a squeak comes out of the horn.

"Try holding your lips tight," says Sally, when she sees what Bev is doing. Bev tries again, but no luck.

"Try blowing harder," says Sally.

Bev blows harder, with her lips tight, and this time she gets out a low note.

"Thanks, Sally," she says. "I'm going to ask Mom and Dad if I can take French horn lessons."

What is the main idea?

Bev wants to play the drums.   Bev blows the horn of the car.

Bev tries to blow the horn.   The horn is hollow.

Gail is taking care of her little sister, Kate. The wind begins to blow hard, and it starts to get dark outside. The sisters look out the window. The sky is a greenish-gray. Suddenly they hear a peal of thunder. The thunder startles Kate and she jumps away from the window.

"Help, Gail!" she cries. "I'm afraid! I don't like thunderstorms!"

Gail goes over to Kate and puts her arms around her. "It's all right," says Gail. "We are safe here inside the house as long as we don't take a bath or use the phone, and stay away from the stove and fridge."

Just then a bright lightning bolt flashes. Gail takes her sister's hand.

"The lightning flashed a long time after the thunder. That means that the thunderstorm is far away, so it is harmless to us."

Kate sighs. "Let's go tell my dolls and stuffed animals that they don't have to be afraid."

What is the main idea?
    __   The thunderstorm is far away.   __   The thunderstorm is close by.

1, 2, 3, 4, or X?
_____ The sisters hear thunder.   _____ Lightning strikes the house.

_____ The lightning flashes.   _____ Gail hugs Kate.

_____ The wind blows hard.   _____ The sky is dark blue.

The woman's _____ is _____ .

mark   bark   Marge   name

Marge has a large _____ of _____ .

hard   glue   jar   good

The dog _____ and _____ .

barked   part   yard   snarled

The farmer has _____ in his _____ .

march   barn   sheep   starve

Marge had lots of _____ at the _____ .

cart   fun   smart   party

There's always something happening at the Paine's farm. In the morning, Mr. Paine feeds oats, hay, and water to the horses, the sheep, and the steer, while Mrs. Paine feeds and waters the goats, chickens, and pigs. After the animals have eaten, Mr. Paine milks the goats and puts the animals out to graze, and his wife lets the chickens out into the barnyard.

For the rest of the day they tend the crops in their garden, and take care of things that need to be fixed. Sometimes the hay needs to be cut and baled; sometimes the sheep need to be sheared.

At night, the chores are the same as the morning, except that the animals have to be led back into the barn for dinner. There's lots of hard work to do on a farm, but Mr. and Mrs. Paine like growing crops and raising animals.

_____

What do the horses eat?   They eat hay and _____

_____

_____ .

barley   corn   bran   oats

Where do the animals sleep?   They sleep in the _____

_____

_____ .

grass   pigpen   barn   barnyard

Jeff and his mom were sitting on the back steps. The sun was setting, and it was getting dark. Jeff saw something sparkling up in the dark sky. He spoke softly:

"Star light, star bright,

First star I see tonight,

I wish I may, I wish I might

Have the wish I wish tonight."

Then he closed his eyes tight and made a wish. But when he looked up, the sparkling light was gone.

"Mom, what happened to the first star?" he asked.

Mom gave him a hug. "That wasn't a star, dear. It was a lightning bug. A lightning bug glows in the dark. It sleeps in the day time and hunts at night."

Jeff looked sad. "Do you think my wish will still come true?" he asked.

Mom smiled. "I bet it will," she told him.

What is the main idea?

Jeff wishes on a star.   The star is sparkling.

Jeff wishes on a lightning bug.   Jeff catches the lightning bug.

_____

_____

_____

_____

Mark and Dee are upstairs playing a game. Dee is running to find a place to hide, and Mark is yelling ". . . four, five, six, here I come!"

Dee wants to hide far away, so she runs downstairs and goes out to the backyard. Mark hears the stairs creaking. "She must be behind the big red easy chair," he says to himself. But he doesn't find her there.

"I've got an idea!" thinks Mark. "Maybe she's out in the car."

He runs out the front door to the driveway. Just as he starts to get in the car, he sees Dee's arm sticking out from behind the corner of the house.

"I see you!" he yells, as he runs to tag her.

What is the main idea?

____ The children play Hide-and-Seek.   ____ Dee is under the stairs.

1, 2, 3, 4, or X?

_____ Mark finds Dee in the den.   _____ Dee runs outside.

_____ Dee hides in the car.   _____ Mark looks downstairs.

_____ Mark finds Dee outside.   _____ The children are upstairs.

Bart saw a huge _____ _____ in the _____ _____ .

sea　　　　shark　　　　hard　　　　either

Dad's _____ _____ is made of _____ _____ cloth.

suit　　　　army　　　　dark　　　　spark

_____ _____ and _____ _____ are men's names.

Marge　　　　Mark　　　　Carl　　　　tar

The dogs _____ _____ in the back _____ _____ .

barked　　　　yarn　　　　partly　　　　yard

The kids _____ _____ at the _____ _____ .

arm　　　　park　　　　play　　　　hard

Deer live all over the U.S.A. They have long, thin legs, short tails, and large, thin ears. Deer can run fast and jump high. They can see, hear, and smell keenly. They eat little plants and buds, twigs, low bushes, moss, tree leaves, and bark.

There are lots of kinds of deer. The white-tailed deer, the black-tailed deer, the elk, the key deer, and the mule deer are five kinds of deer.

The male deer are named bucks, or stags. They grow big horns or antlers made of bone. Each winter they shed the antlers, and each spring they grow back. At first the antlers are soft, but then they grow hard as a rock. The doe is the female deer. Most female deer don't have antlers.

_____

What is the male deer called?   He is called a _____

_____

_____ .

black-tailed   doe   buck   antler

When does the deer shed the antlers?   He sheds them in the _____

_____

_____ .

spring   summer   winter   daytime

Seals are animals that live in the sea. They can be between three and sixteen feet long. Their shape is streamlined, like a racing car, so that they can swim fast. In place of arms and legs, they have short flippers. Their back flippers help them steer when they swim, like fish's tails.

Lots of times seals like to swim on their backs. When they are on the shore, they get from place to place by inching forward on their bellies. In Maine, you can see seals sitting on rock ledges in the sun, but they are scared of people, so if they hear you go by in a boat they will jump back into the sea.

Seals have a layer of thick fat under their skin to keep them from getting cold in the sea. This fat is called blubber.

Seals' ears don't show the way people's ears do. They are just little holes.

Some seals, mainly babies, make a bleating sound; some snarl and bark, and some roar.

What is the main idea?

Seals are reptiles.   Seals are suited to the sea.

Seals have flippers.   Blubber keeps seals cold.

Carly held the ladder against the oak tree while Mark carried up a large board.

"This is the last board for the north wall," Mark said as he nailed the board to the treehouse. Carly followed him up the steps.

"We can see really far from here. I bet this is the tallest treehouse around," she said. "We can see all the way down to the corner store!"

"Yup," said Mark. "And we can spy on Bobby, next door." They both giggled at that idea.

"Kids! Supper!" Dad called from the back door.

"Let's ask if we can eat up here," said Carly, as she started down the ladder.

"Good idea," said Mark, close behind her.

Dad said OK, and gave them dinner on a tray. They stayed in the treehouse until dark.

_____

What is the main idea?

___ Dad said the treehouse was not safe.   ___ The children used the treehouse.

1, 2, 3, 4, or X?

_____ They ate dinner up there.   _____ Carly held the board.

_____ The ladder fell down.   _____ Carly followed him.

_____ Mark went up the ladder.   _____ The children looked around.

Dad drove the _____ to the _____ .

_____   _____

part   car   farm   scar

Carl and _____ play _____ .

_____   _____

cards   Marty   sharp   snarl

Mom _____ the car in the back _____ .

_____   _____

parks   carve   yard   shark

_____ said that the test was _____ .

_____   _____

partly   starve   hard   Bart

The _____ will _____ at six o'clock.

_____   _____

little   after   start   party

Robby wants to be an artist when he grows up. He has been taking art lessons on weekends since March. His art class is going to have a show of paintings on Sunday morning in the parking lot next to the art school.

On Sunday morning, Robby goes to help his art teacher set up the show. They string cord from one corner of the lot to another; then they hang the paintings on the cord. Robby's painting is a large seascape, with some sailboats in a harbor and a white lighthouse on the shore. He made the sky light blue and the grass on the shore dark green. His painting is in a gold frame and has a tan mat.

Robby was pleased that his mother and father came to the show.

"I like your painting," said Dad. "I feel like I can smell the sea."

"Me, too," added Mom. "It looks like you worked hard on it."

Where was the art show?   It was in _____

_____

_____ .

Robby's house   the parking lot   a lighthouse   the art store

When was the art show?   It was _____

_____

_____ .

all weekend   on Sunday   March 3   for three days

It is the end of the school year, so Mark is having a party. He invites some friends to go for a hayride. When they get to the farm, they see a cart filled with hay, and the farmer hitching a mule up to the cart.

"Where is the black horse that pulled the cart last time?" Mark asks the farmer.

"He has a sore leg," the farmer tells him. "Jump in."

The farmer tries to get the mule to walk on the road, but the mule won't budge. It smells the hay in the cart and keeps trying to eat it.

The angry farmer starts hollering, but then he gets an idea. He grabs a handful of hay from the cart and runs in front of the mule. The mule sees the hay and starts to walk to get it.

"Yippee!" cheer the children in the cart, as the hayride begins.

What is the main idea?

The black horse pulls the cart.   The mule eats all the hay.

The cart tips over.   The hayride starts late.

Lee walked into the den where Dad was reading.

"Look at my blue jeans," he said, holding them up to show Dad. "I have worn them so much that there are holes in the knees. But I've had them for so long and I like them so much that I don't want to throw them out."

"Well," said Dad, taking the jeans from Lee and holding them up to see the holes, "We can either patch them or we can make shorts out of them by cutting off the torn part. Which do you want to do?"

"Summer's coming, so I'll vote for the shorts," replied Lee.

Dad went into the kitchen for a little while and came back with a pair of blue shorts, which he handed to Lee.

"Thanks, Dad," said Lee. "These shorts are neat."

What is the main idea?

   __ Dad patches Lee's jeans.   __ Lee gets a pair of shorts.

1, 2, 3, 4, or X?

_____ Lee shows Dad his jeans.   _____ Dad gets shorts at the store.

_____ Dad cuts off the legs of the jeans.   _____ Dad puts a patch on the holes.

_____ Dad takes the jeans to the   _____ Dad hands the shorts to Lee.

       kitchen.

The _____ ripped Carl's _____ .

    wore   shorts   thorn   north

Mr. Carter's first _____ is _____ .

    snore   Norm   Marge   name

The colt was _____ in the _____ .

    sport   morning   marking   born

The _____ of jam has a _____ in it.

    jar   boring   cork   torn

It was snowing _____ in the _____ .

    hard   storm   score   worn

As Pete and his dad rowed out of the harbor at Black Bay, Pete suddenly yelled, "Look! There's a cork floating over there in the water. Maybe it's stuck in a bottle!"

Dad rowed over to where the cork was bobbing up and down in the waves. Pete reached into the bay.

"I've got it," he said. "It's stuck in a jar, and there's a note in it."

Dad pulled the oars into the boat. "What does the note say?" he asked.

Pete unfolded the note and began to read it. It said, "If you find this note, you will have good luck. I am a fisherman. DMC. March, 1980."

"Just think! That bottle has been bobbing around in the sea all that time!" said Pete. "I hope the note comes true!"

_____

When was the note written?   The note was written _____

_____

_____ .

last week   a year ago   last year   in 1980

Where did Pete see the cork?   Pete saw the cork in the _____

_____

_____ .

blue bottle   bay   Black Sea   stream

Norm mows the grass in Mr. Forman's yard each weekend. It's the biggest yard Norm mows, but he charges Mr. Forman just ten dollars, which is a good deal.

Last weekend there was a bad rainstorm. It rained off and on for three days, so Norm had to wait to do the mowing. At last, on Tuesday, the sky cleared and it was sunny. By two o'clock, the grass had dried and was fine to mow.

Mr. Forman was not home when Norm did the job. The grass had grown a lot, so it was hard to mow, but Norm tried his best. After he got that done, he clipped the tall grass next to the house.

At four o'clock, Mr. Forman came to pay Norm.

"Thanks for doing the clipping," he said. "The yard looks really nice."

He handed Norm twelve dollars and Norm was pleased.

What is the main idea?

Norm clips and mows the grass.   Mr. Forman comes home.

Norm gets four dollars.   The rainstorm lasts four weeks.

Beavers have wide, flat tails that help them in lots of ways. When they are using their sharp teeth to cut down trees for their lodges, they stand on their two short legs and use their tails to support themselves. In this case, the tail is like a third leg. It keeps the beaver from falling over when he is biting at the tree trunk.

Beavers' tails also come in handy when they are swimming. They use their tails like paddles to help them steer as they swim.

Lastly, beavers slap the mud with their tails when they want to send other beavers a warning.

What is the main idea?

___ Beavers' tails are useful.   ___ Beavers are smart animals.

1, 2, 3, 4, or X?

_____ They use logs for their lodges.   _____ Beavers wag their tails at friends.

_____ They use their tails while   _____ Beavers use their tails to support
swimming.   themselves.

_____ They chase otters with their tails.   _____ They slap their tails as a signal.

The _____ has a _____ mane and a tail.

cord   short   fork   horse

They ate _____ and _____ for dinner.

park   cards   pork   corn

Baseball is a _____ for the _____ .

summer   sport   snort   start

Carl _____ a pair of _____ .

fort   wore   horn   shorts

The puppy _____ when it _____ .

boring   snores   sleeps   cart

March 30—I went to the store and got a packet of corn seeds.

May 20—I dug up a garden in the backyard.

May 24—I planted a row of corn seeds in the garden.

May 31—Little green buds started to show.

June 15—I thinned out the weakest plants and left the strongest ones there to grow.

June 20—It hasn't rained in days, so I had to water the garden with the hose.

September 1—I picked my first batch of corn. Some friends came over for dinner. We had corn on the cob and baked fish. It was yummy.

September 15—I chased a deer out of the garden. He bit the tops off the two biggest plants!

September 20—I've had corn on the cob for dinner fifteen times since September 1.

September 22—A frost came and killed all the corn plants. Next year I'll plant corn again—and maybe I'll plant popcorn seeds, too!

—Mrs. Campbell

_____

_____

What did Mrs. Campbell thin out?   She thinned out the _____

_____

_____ plants.

strongest   weakest   tallest   shortest

_____

Who or what killed the corn plants?   _____

_____

_____ killed them.

Mrs. Campbell   A deer   Friends   Frost

About five hundred years ago, in a time called the Middle Ages, kings and queens ruled the lands. They were so rich that they had hundreds of people working for them.

All the land belonged to the king. He hired people called lords to take care of the land for him. He gave the lords castles to live in, and then the lords hired the poorest people to farm the land. The poor people had to give all the crops to the lord and the king.

The king also hired men called knights to protect him and his queen. The knights wore silver armor and carried spears in case they had to fight in a duel or a battle for the king.

The king and queen lived in a huge castle that needed many people to keep it clean and in order. There were gate-keepers, maids, butchers, tailors, blacksmiths, candle-makers, people to tend the moat, and many more. The king even had a jester—a man who danced, did tricks, and told jokes just to make the king happy.

What is the main idea?

The king worked at many jobs.   Many people worked for the king.

The Middle Ages hasn't happened yet.   In the Middle Ages there were butchers.

_____

_____

_____

_____

Fran is sweeping the barn when she hears a "Clip, clop." She looks up and sees her horse trotting out of the open door of his stall.

She grabs a rope and runs to catch the horse, but he canters away. She looks up and down and all around the road, but she does not see him, so she rides her bike to the farms nearby to see if he is there. No luck. Fran hunts and hunts, but she still can't find him.

After a while it starts to get dark. Fran says to herself, "I think I'd better get some help." She goes back to the barn. And there she finds her horse, standing in his stall waiting for her.

What is the main idea?

— The dog runs away.   — The horse plays a joke.

1, 2, 3, 4, or X?

_____ Fran hunts for her horse.   _____ Fran finds her horse standing in

_____ Fran sees her horse at a nearby   the barn.

   farm.   _____ Fran smiles at her horse.

_____ Fran is sweeping the barn.   _____ The horse trots out of the barn.

The girl _____ off the _____ .

       stir   turns   fur   T.V.

The boy's _____ name is _____ .

       dirt   first   Kurt   chirp

Pete ate the _____ with _____ on it.

       ketchup   burger   shirt   thirsty

Ed _____ the _____ that he made.

       bird   chilly   shirt   wore

The dog naps in a _____ in the _____ .

       sir   firm   hole   dirt

Fern lives with her mom, but she sees her dad on Thursdays and on weekends. This Thursday is Fern's birthday.

"Where do you want to go for your birthday dinner?" asks Dad when he picks her up on Thursday at three-thirty.

"The burger place," replies Fern, and off they go.

"I think I'll try the turkey sandwich this time," says Dad as they reach the drive-up window, "but you order first. Order what you want." Fern leans out the window.

"Beef burger, large order of French fries, and a cherry milkshake, please. And do you have birthday cake? Today is my birthday." The girl who is taking the order smiles.

"We don't have cake, but I'll see what I can do." After a while she comes back with Fran's order, plus a free apple pie with a candle in the middle of it.

"Happy Birthday!" she tells Fran.

_____

What does Fran get to eat?   She gets a _____

_____

_____ .

cheeseburger   beef burger   turkey sandwich   cake

Who orders the turkey sandwich? _____

_____

_____ orders it.

Mom   Fern   Dad   The girl

The turtle is a reptile that lives inside a hard shell made of bone. You can tell how old a turtle is by counting the rings on the shell, but it is sometimes hard to see the rings.

Turtles don't have teeth, so they cannot cut or grind food. They eat small insects, worms, snails, slugs, and crayfish, and they drink a lot of water.

Some turtles live just on land, some live just in the sea or lakes, and some live on land and in water. Land turtles are the slowest and most clumsy. They have short legs and stubby feet and are not good fighters, so they need their shells to hide in.

All turtles lay their eggs on land, in a nest in a sunny place. They tend to live for a long time. They are strong, and if they are hurt it doesn't take them long to get better.

What is the main idea?

Turtles can have a hundred rings.   Turtles are weak animals.

Turtles are reptiles.   Some turtles live in the sea.

_____

_____

_____

_____

Ms. Carter came marching into the house. "There's something wrong with my car," she said to her stepson, Marco. "I can't get it to start. When I turn the key, I don't hear a thing."

"I'll see what I can do," said Marco, who was sixteen years old. He stopped doing his homework and followed her out to the driveway. "It might be a wet wire from the rainstorm, or maybe it's the spark plugs."

He looked inside the front. "I think I see what the problem is," he said right away. "See all that white junk on those wires?" he asked. "The battery can't charge with all that stuff all over it."

He cleaned the messy wire and put them back on the battery. "Try to start the car again, he said.

Ms. Carter got in the car and turned the key. The car started right away. "Thanks, Marco," she said. "I'm glad you know about cars!"

What is the main idea?

   — Marco helps his stepmother.   — Marco watches TV.

1, 2, 3, 4, or X?

_____ Ms. Carter fixes her own car.   _____ The car starts.

_____ The spark plugs are bad.   _____ Ms. Carter asks Marco for help.

_____ Marco fixes the car.   _____ The car won't start.

The two _____ _____ are swimming in the _____ .

jerk   girls   surf   germ

Some people go to _____ _____ on _____ _____ .

church   turtle   Sunday   fir

That _____ _____ is a _____ _____ dumb bird.

enter   large   thunder   turkey

_____ _____ is the _____ _____ oldest child in the class.

burro   Bert   third   stir

Kurt _____ _____ the cake mix _____ _____ the TV show.

during   lantern   birch   stirred

Jenny had been waiting up all night to see her mare give birth to its first foal, but at about five in the morning she fell asleep by the stall.

She woke up to a surprise. A black colt was lying in the hay, and the mare was licking him dry. His wet mane and tail were curly, and his hair was shiny with wetness. He had a white star in the middle of his face.

"I'll name you Star," said Jenny. "Happy birthday, Star."

Then the colt began to stand up—or at least he <u>tried</u> to stand up. He stretched out his front feet first, but they were too wobbly. By the time he picked up his back feet, his front feet buckled under, and he fell down—plop—in the hay. The colt snorted. Then he tried again.

"Come on, Star! You can do it!" cheered Jenny. And this time he did.

_____

                                                    _____
What part of the foal had white on it?   The foal had white on its _____

_____

_____ .

face   legs   mane   tail

                                            _____
Where was the foal?   It was in the _____

_____

_____ .

grass   house   hay   stars

78

Squirrels are furry gray animals with big, thick bushy tails that they can curl around them to keep warm. They have strong hind legs to help them get up trees and jump from branch to branch. Their teeth are strong, too, so they can crush nuts and seeds.

Squirrels live in hollow tree trunks or in the branches of trees, where they make their nests. They gather leaves, twigs, or bits of dried bark to put in their nests to make them soft.

Squirrels do other gathering, too. Since they stay in their nests in the winter, in the fall they collect corn, berries, nuts, or seeds and store them to eat during the cold. You may have seen squirrels gathering acorns and putting them inside their cheeks to take back to their nests.

What is the main idea?

Squirrels do their gathering in the winter.   Squirrels have curly tails.

Squirrels have lots to do.   Squirrels jump in trees.

Kay is watching Dad make popcorn in the popcorn maker they just got at the hardware store. First he pours in the kernels. Then he puts the top on the popcorn maker and turns it on.

Kay watches the window on the side of the popcorn maker. Inside, the hot air begins to blow. A fan blows the kernels around in circles so they don't burn on the bottom. After a while, the first kernel bursts. The sudden POP startles Kay, and she jumps. Then lots of other kernels begin to pop. The corn is whirling and spinning in the hot air. Before long, the popped kernels fill up the popcorn maker. Dad puts a dab of butter in the top of the lid to melt, and turns it off.

"Get a big bowl, Kay," he says. "This is going to be a treat!"

What is the main idea?

— Kay pops the popcorn.   — Kay watches Dad make popcorn.

1, 2, 3, 4, or X?

_____ The butter gets too hot.   _____ Dad pours in the kernels.

_____ The kernels burst.   _____ He turns on the popcorn maker.

_____ The kernels whirl in the air.   _____ Kay eats all the popcorn.

Flora saw a _____ of _____ .

hard   horses   enter   herd

Herb drops the _____ in the mail _____ .

box   ladder   teacher   letter

The _____ wore a blue _____ .

girl   dirt   skirt   burn

Carlos will be _____ on his next _____ .

pork   thirteen   bunny   birthday

The _____ put ice on Dan's _____ .

silly   nurse   burn   thirty

Herb sat on the train to Denver looking out the window. He was going to visit his uncle. This was a three-day trip, so he saw all kinds of sights. He saw skyscrapers, trees, cliffs, rainbows, farms, barns, blue sky, and green farm land. He saw burros, turkeys, wild deer, and steer roaming the western plains.

On the last day of the trip Herb saw the best sight of all. As the train speeded along a wide, flat plain there was a herd of wild horses grazing not far from the tracks. When the train passed by, the horses lifted their tails in the air and began to buck and snort. Then the leader of the herd began to gallop alongside the train, and the rest of the herd followed—black, gray, white, and spotted horses all running next to the train.

"The horses seem to be racing with the train," Herb said to himself. "I hope they win!"

_____

Where was Herb going?   He was going to _____

_____

_____ .

the west coast   the east coast   a horse farm   Denver

What did the horses do?   They _____

_____

_____ .

saw Herb   raced the train   chased the steer   rolled over

Kurt Carver is a state cop. Tonight he is in a cruiser, parked between two birch trees on the side of the highway, watching for cars that are speeding.

Before long, a little red sports car races by at top speed. Kurt turns on the blue and white lights on the top of the cruiser and takes off after it. At first, the driver doesn't see the lights flashing behind him, or maybe he just doesn't want to stop. He passes a van, then veers back into the right lane.

But Kurt follows right behind him. At last, the driver turns off the highway and screeches to a halt. Kurt stops his car, gets out, and gives the driver a speeding ticket.

"You've got to slow down," he says to the man, "or you're going to hurt someone."

_____

What is the main idea?

      The sports car hits the cruiser.   Kurt catches the speeder.

      The sports car is red.   The speeder gets away.

_____

_____

_____

_____

Bert asked Dee to go to the square dance with him on Thursday night. Dee was pleased. It was her first time at a square dance. She liked braiding her hair and dressing up in a long purple skirt. When Bert came to pick her up, he looked handsome in his checked shirt and blue jeans. He told her how nice she looked.

The barn was packed full of people when Bert and Dee walked in, and things were really lively. Mr. Hammond and Mr. Kirk were playing fiddle, and Mrs. Beatly was calling the dances. Men and women were in a circle, holding hands, then dancing arm in arm in pairs, then twirling and whirling around with their partners.

"Shall we dance?" asked Bert, as he put out his arm to Dee.

"Let's," replied Dee, and they walked on to the dance floor.

What is the main idea?

   — Dee and Bert look nice.   — Dee and Bert go dancing.

1, 2, 3, 4, or X?

_____ Dee gets dressed up.   _____ They go to the barn.

_____ Bert asks Dee to go dancing.   _____ Mrs. Beatly plays the fiddle.

_____ Bert and Dee dance.   _____ Mr. Hammond plays the flute.

The _____ gets _____ prize.

first   squirm   winner   during

The _____ was _____ in the nest.

manners   bird   chirping   shirt

The girl kicked the _____ with her _____ .

curl   spare   horse   spurs

Kurt put on his _____ and _____ .

robe   third   slippers   curve

The _____ and _____ will help the hurt boy.

twirl   nurse   snarl   doctor

Bart made a birdfeeder in carpentry class. His mother and father hung it outside the kitchen window. Bart was excited when the first sparrow arrived and began pecking at the birdseed. Soon there was hardly any birdseed left in the feeder.

"Those sparrows really eat fast!" exclaimed Bart. But just then two squirrels scampered up the trunk of the tree and jumped across onto the feeder.

"I think the squirrels are the ones who ate all that birdseed," said his father. "We'd better think of a way to keep them out of the feeder."

"I've got an idea," said Bart. He got two plastic plates from the kitchen cupboard and poked holes in them. Then he hung one on top of the birdfeeder and the other underneath it. After a while, a squirrel crept up the tree and jumped across to the birdfeeder. But this time he landed on the slippery plastic plate and slid off. The next time he tried to go down the rope the feeder was hanging from, but the other plate was in the way.

"It looks like you solved the squirrel problem," said his father. Before long, the sparrows had returned.

_____

Where did Mother and Father put the feeder?   They put it in the _____

_____

_____ .

in the birch tree   in the maple tree   carpentry class   outside the window

Who put the plates up? _____

_____

_____ put the plates up.

Father   Bart   Mother   Squirrels

Kurt had his first sailing lesson when he was at camp this summer. In fact, it was his first time in a boat and he was surprised at how tippy it was. The sailing teacher told him to be careful as he stepped off the dock into the boat.

"You are sitting in the stern of the boat. It means the back," the teacher told him. "And that curved stick you are holding is called the rudder. The rudder of the boat is like the steering wheel of a car, except for one thing. In a sailboat, when you want to go to the right you push the rudder to the left. And we don't say the 'right' in a boat; we say 'starboard.' And we call the left the 'port.'

"Now let's put up the sail. This rope is connected to a pulley. Pull the rope down and the sail will go up."

"This is very confusing," Kurt said. "I'm afraid I'll forget it all."

"Don't worry," said the teacher. "Sailing may seem hard at first, but I bet you'll catch on fast."

What is the main idea?

Kurt falls off the boat.   The boat has a pulley.

Kurt turns the boat.   Kurt has a sailing lesson.

_____

_____

_____

_____

Marge's thirteenth birthday was on Tuesday, March 10. Five girls came over to her house at three-thirty and gave her a surprise party. Marge had taken her sister to her painting class, and when she came back the girls all burst out singing HAPPY BIRTHDAY! They had ice cream and a cake with thirteen candles on it—plus one to grow on! The candles were the kind that sparkle in the dark. A pile of cards and gifts was in the corner.

After they had cake and ice cream, Marge turned to the pile of cards and gifts. "I'm going to read all the cards to you," she said. "They are really cute."

Marge liked her gifts. There was a pair of wild boxer shorts, a fancy blue silk shirt, and a mirror with a silver border and handle. Three girls pitched in and got her a hair dryer. And last, but not least, was a card from Mom and Dad which said, "Next Thursday we will take you to the hairdresser, and you can have a perm."

Her first perm! Marge felt so grown-up on her thirteenth birthday—her first day as a teen.

What is the main idea?

___ Marge ate cake.   ___ Marge had a birthday surprise.

1, 2, 3, 4, or X?

_____ Marge felt grown-up.   _____ Marge got a cake.

_____ The party was on Thursday.   _____ Marge had her third birthday.

_____ Five friends came to Marge's house.   _____ She got cards and gifts.

A _____ is _____ next to the tree.

fern   sparkle   worm   growing

The _____ leaped onto the _____ .

firm   birdfeeder   purple   squirrel

The dog's _____ is _____ and black.

sir   during   fur   curly

The girl reads the first _____ of the _____ .

poem   verse   church   third

Kurt's _____ gave him a _____ .

Thursday   stir   friend   surprise

The eagle is one of the largest, strongest birds there is. Eagles' wing span can be as long as 8 feet. That means that when they hold out their wings, it is 8 feet from the tip of one wing to another. They can soar high in the air with these large wings.

Their toes are sharp and their beaks are quite strong, with the top part curling down over the bottom part. This shape helps them when they hunt. Sometimes eagles hunt small birds, but they are so big and strong that they can hunt rabbits, sheep, and deer, too.

An eagle makes its nest high up on the steep cliffs or in branches in tall trees so they will be safe. Their nests, called aeries (ayr-eez), can be as big as six feet wide.

_____

What do eagles hunt?   Eagles hunt _____

_____

_____ .

condors   smaller birds   larger birds   people

What are aeries?   Aeries are the eagles' _____

_____

_____ .

wing span   eggs   nests   curved beaks

The TV in Ms. Parker's den is on, but she isn't watching it. She's thirsty, so she's in the kitchen getting a drink of water. Her dog, Duke, is sleeping in the den.

Suddenly, Ms. Parker hears Duke barking. She thinks someone may be at the front door or outside the window, so she goes and checks, but no one is around. Duke starts barking again.

Ms. Parker walks back to the den to see why he is barking. Duke is on the rug and his fur is standing up on end. When she sees the TV, Ms. Parker begins to grin. There is a dog barking on the screen. Duke must think it's a real dog!

She turns off the TV and pats Duke. "That isn't a real dog," she tells him. "He won't hurt you."

Duke looks puzzled.

What is the main idea?

Duke barks at the TV.   Ms. Parker gets a drink.

The dog barks at the squirrel.   The dogs get into a fight.

Norm was making three hamburgers—one for Mom, one for Dad, and one for himself. First he got the hamburger out of the fridge, and then he split it up into three piles. He shaped each pile into a round ball with his hands, then pressed on each ball to flatten it.

Next Norm turned on the burner to heat up the frying pan, and then set the burgers in it. He started with the heat up high, and then turned it down to keep the burgers from burning. While the burgers were frying, he toasted three buns. He set out a jar of pickles, a jar of mustard, and a bottle of ketchup. He turned each burger over, and got glasses for grape juice. Then he turned off the stove and put each burger on a bun.

"Lunch is served," he told Mom and Dad, who were in the hall fixing a hole in the plaster.

"What a nice surprise," said Dad when he saw lunch all made.

What is the main idea?

    __ Norm made lunch.   __ Norm made dinner.

1, 2, 3, 4, or X?

_____ Norm toasted the buns.   _____ Norm made four burgers.

_____ He turned on the burner.   _____ He served the burgers.

_____ Mom made beef pot pies.   _____ Norm shaped the hamburgers.

The _____ sat on a _____ in its cage.

bird   perch   Bert   burst

The man is _____ years _____ .

thirty   first   old   whirl

A _____ has soft _____ leaves.

germ   green   jerk   fern

Mom keeps her _____ in her _____ .

nurse   purse   cash   during

Mrs. Burns wore a long _____ to the _____ .

stir   party   spurt   skirt

Dolphins are sleek animals that live in seas and rivers. They look like small whales, growing up to twelve feet long, and are black on top and white below. They have flippers, a big fin on their backs, and a flat tail fin. They have lots of sharp teeth, and eat mostly fish. Dolphins can swim fast, and like to come up for air and bob around. They are playful animals. Out in bays they sometimes follow boats and jump up in the air behind the sterns. They don't seem to be afraid of people, and they look as if they are saying hello and having a good time.

Dolphins are quite smart. They make sounds—whistles, barks, and clicks—which seem to mean something. They are perfect subjects for people to watch and try to understand. People like dolphins. Some people think that when schools, or herds, of dolphins appear near ships as they sail out of the harbor, it means that the ship will have a good trip.

_____

Where do dolphins live?   They live in _____

_____

_____ .

boats   North Bay   the sea   lakes

How big are dolphins?   Dolphins can grow up to _____

_____

_____ feet long.

a hundred   a thousand   twelve   four

"Good luck," says Mom to Kay, as Kay tightens the laces on her skates. But Kay barely hears her. It's her first time skating in a show, and her nerves are on edge. She adjusts the strap of her fur hat and waits for her turn. Her hands are shaking.

Then Kay hears her name. "I hope people can't see me shaking," she thinks.

She starts by skating around in a circle, first on one foot and then on two. The blades on her skates are so sharp that they scratch a perfect circle into the ice. People cheer, but Kay doesn't hear them. Her mind is all on skating. Now she is no longer shaking.

She leans on one skate and holds her other toe in her hand. Then she bends down on one knee, tips her head back, and holds her arms out at each side. Her turn is over.

At last Kay hears the cheering and clapping! She is so glad it's over and that she did a good job that she bursts into happy tears as soon as she steps off the ice.

What is the main idea?

Kay falls on the ice.   Kay tightens her skates.

Kay does a good job.   Kay twirls and spins.

The flurries started as the sun set behind the big brick church. A layer of snow dusted cars, streets, and sidewalks. Before he went to bed, five-year-old Bert looked out at the lightly falling snow.

As he snuggled under his blanket and quilt he started thinking about what he wanted to do in the morning if there was no school. Maybe he'd sleep late. No. He'd get up at six and see if the snow was good for sledding. If it looked like it was deep, he'd have some juice, an oat bran muffin, and a glass of milk. Then he'd call his friend Carl and see if he wanted to go over to the park to go sledding. If he did, he'd get out his sled and meet Carl at the corner.

Drifting off to sleep, Bert dreamed he was whizzing down the hill, with the snow swirling all around him.

What is the main idea?

___ Bert wants to go sledding.   ___ Bert is sleeping late.

1, 2, 3, 4, or X?

_____ Bert fell out of bed.   _____ He dreamed he was whizzing

_____ The flurries were falling.   down the hill.

_____ Bert went to bed.   _____ He'd get up at six.

_____ He cleared off the snow.